My Emotions Journal

A daily personal journal

Based on the "My Emotions" book
by My Skills Books

My Skills Books | myskillsbooks.com

Copyright © 2025 by My Skills Books

Published by My Skills Books

All rights reserved. No part of this publication may be reproduced, distributed, or transmitted in any form or by any means, including photocopying, recording, or other electronic or mechanical methods, without the prior written permission of the publisher, except in the case of brief quotations embodied in critical reviews and certain other noncommercial uses permitted by copyright law.

First Printing, 2025.

ISBN: 978-1-951573-56-0

www.myskillsbooks.com

How do you feel today?

Date: / /   Journal Entry

_____
_____
_____
_____
_____
_____
_____
_____
_____
_____
_____
_____
_____
_____
_____
_____
_____
_____
_____
_____
_____
_____

How do you feel today?

Date: / /   Journal Entry

_____
_____
_____
_____
_____
_____
_____
_____
_____
_____
_____
_____
_____
_____
_____
_____
_____
_____
_____
_____

How do you feel today?

Date: / /   Journal Entry

How do you feel today?

Date: /   /   Journal Entry

How do you feel today?

Date: /   /   Journal Entry

How do you feel today?

Date: /   /   Journal Entry

How do you feel today?

Date: /   /   Journal Entry

Date: / / Journal Entry

How do you feel today?

Date: /   /   Journal Entry

_____
_____
_____
_____
_____
_____
_____
_____
_____
_____
_____
_____
_____
_____
_____
_____
_____
_____
_____

How do you feel today?

Date: /   /   Journal Entry

_____
_____
_____
_____
_____
_____
_____
_____
_____
_____
_____
_____
_____
_____
_____
_____
_____
_____
_____
_____

How do you feel today?

Date: /   /   Journal Entry

_____
_____
_____
_____
_____
_____
_____
_____
_____
_____
_____
_____
_____
_____
_____
_____
_____
_____
_____
_____

How do you feel today?

Date: / /   Journal Entry

_____
_____
_____
_____
_____
_____
_____
_____
_____
_____
_____
_____
_____
_____
_____
_____
_____
_____

How do you feel today?

Date: /   /   Journal Entry

___
___
___
___
___
___
___
___
___
___
___
___
___
___
___
___
___
___
___

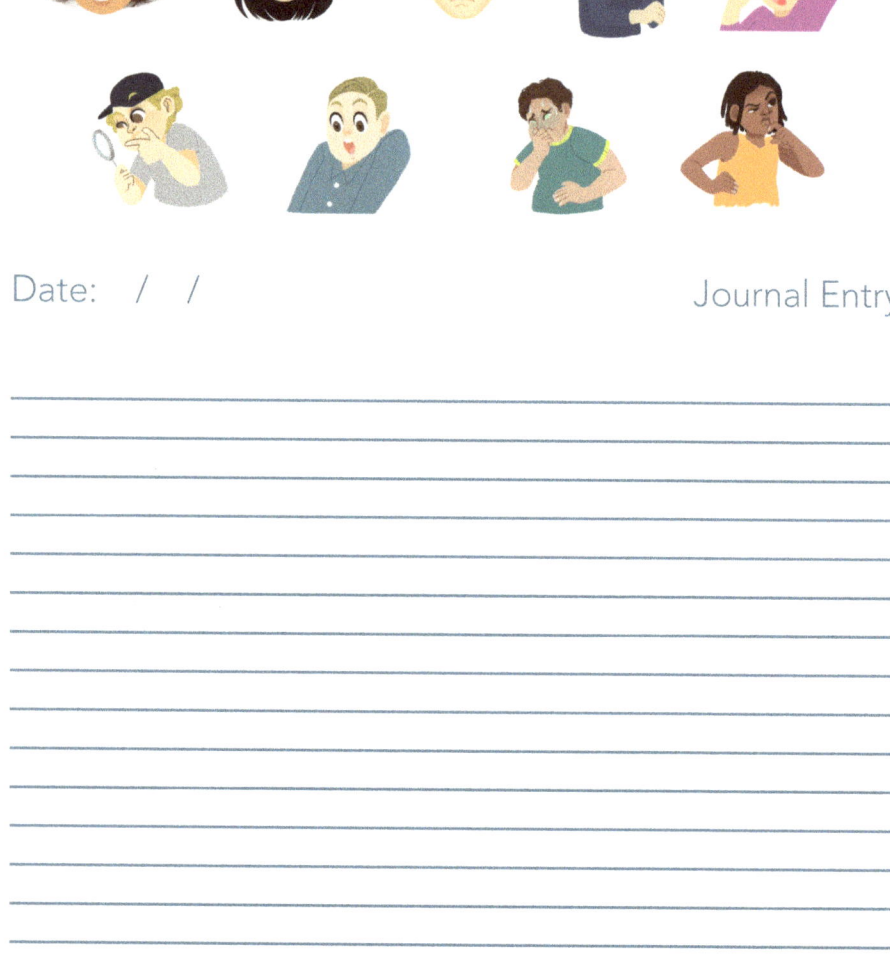

Date: / /   Journal Entry

How do you feel today?

Date: /   /   Journal Entry

_____
_____
_____
_____
_____
_____
_____
_____
_____
_____
_____
_____
_____
_____
_____
_____
_____
_____
_____
_____
_____

Date: / /

Journal Entry

How do you feel today?

Date: / /   Journal Entry

_____
_____
_____
_____
_____
_____
_____
_____
_____
_____
_____
_____
_____
_____
_____
_____
_____
_____
_____
_____
_____

How do you feel today?

Date: /   /   Journal Entry

_____
_____
_____
_____
_____
_____
_____
_____
_____
_____
_____
_____
_____
_____
_____
_____
_____
_____
_____
_____

How do you feel today?

Date: / /   Journal Entry

Date: / /

Journal Entry

How do you feel today?

Date: / /   Journal Entry

How do you feel today?

Date: / /   Journal Entry

Date: /   /   Journal Entry

How do you feel today?

Date: /   /   Journal Entry

_____
_____
_____
_____
_____
_____
_____
_____
_____
_____
_____
_____
_____
_____
_____
_____
_____
_____
_____

How do you feel today?

Date: /   /   Journal Entry

___
___
___
___
___
___
___
___
___
___
___
___
___
___
___
___
___
___
___
___
___

Date: / /

Journal Entry

How do you feel today?

Date: / /   Journal Entry

_____
_____
_____
_____
_____
_____
_____
_____
_____
_____
_____
_____
_____
_____
_____
_____
_____
_____
_____
_____

How do you feel today?

Date: / /   Journal Entry

How do you feel today?

Date: /   /   Journal Entry

How do you feel today?

Date: / /   Journal Entry

_____
_____
_____
_____
_____
_____
_____
_____
_____
_____
_____
_____
_____
_____
_____
_____
_____
_____
_____
_____

How do you feel today?

Date: / /   Journal Entry

Date: / /

Journal Entry

How do you feel today?

Date: / /   Journal Entry

_____
_____
_____
_____
_____
_____
_____
_____
_____
_____
_____
_____
_____
_____
_____
_____
_____
_____
_____
_____
_____
_____

How do you feel today?

Date: /   /   Journal Entry

_____
_____
_____
_____
_____
_____
_____
_____
_____
_____
_____
_____
_____
_____
_____
_____
_____
_____
_____
_____
_____
_____
_____

Date: /   /   Journal Entry

How do you feel today?

Date: / /   Journal Entry

How do you feel today?

Date: /   /   Journal Entry

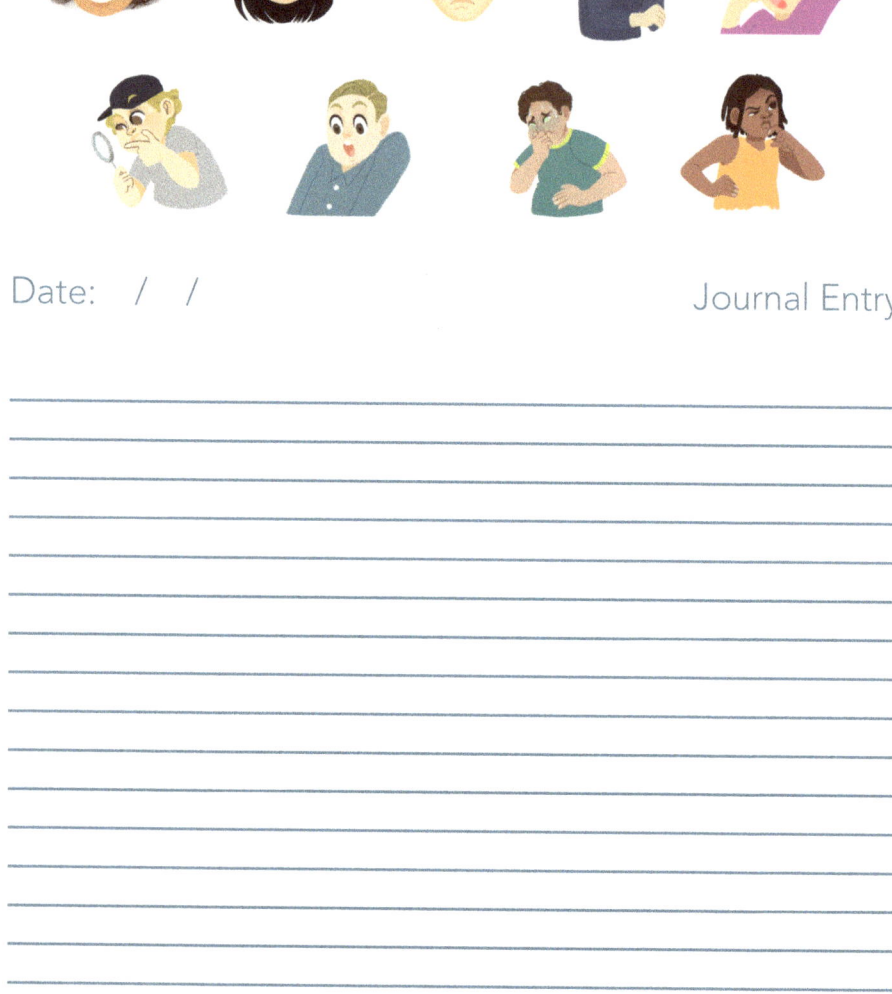

How do you feel today?

Date: /   /   Journal Entry

_____
_____
_____
_____
_____
_____
_____
_____
_____
_____
_____
_____
_____
_____
_____
_____
_____
_____

How do you feel today?

Date: /   /   Journal Entry

_____
_____
_____
_____
_____
_____
_____
_____
_____
_____
_____
_____
_____
_____
_____
_____
_____
_____
_____

How do you feel today?

Date: /   /   Journal Entry

How do you feel today?

Date: / /   Journal Entry

How do you feel today?

Date: / /   Journal Entry

Date: / /

Journal Entry

How do you feel today?

Date: /   /   Journal Entry

_____
_____
_____
_____
_____
_____
_____
_____
_____
_____
_____
_____
_____
_____
_____
_____
_____
_____
_____
_____

How do you feel today?

Date: /   /   Journal Entry

How do you feel today?

Date: /   /   Journal Entry

_____
_____
_____
_____
_____
_____
_____
_____
_____
_____
_____
_____
_____
_____
_____
_____
_____
_____

How do you feel today?

Date: /   /   Journal Entry

How do you feel today?

Date: / /   Journal Entry

Date: / /   Journal Entry

How do you feel today?

Date: / /   Journal Entry

Date: / /

Journal Entry

How do you feel today?

Date: /   /   Journal Entry

How do you feel today?

Date: /   /   Journal Entry

_____
_____
_____
_____
_____
_____
_____
_____
_____
_____
_____
_____
_____
_____
_____
_____
_____
_____
_____
_____

How do you feel today?

Date: / /   Journal Entry

_____
_____
_____
_____
_____
_____
_____
_____
_____
_____
_____
_____
_____
_____
_____
_____
_____
_____

How do you feel today?

Date: /   /   Journal Entry

How do you feel today?

Date: / /   Journal Entry

_____
_____
_____
_____
_____
_____
_____
_____
_____
_____
_____
_____
_____
_____
_____
_____
_____
_____
_____
_____

How do you feel today?

Date: / /   Journal Entry

How do you feel today?

Date: / /   Journal Entry

How do you feel today?

Date: /   /   Journal Entry

Date: / /   Journal Entry

Date: /   /   Journal Entry

How do you feel today?

Date: / /   Journal Entry

_____
_____
_____
_____
_____
_____
_____
_____
_____
_____
_____
_____
_____
_____
_____
_____
_____
_____
_____
_____
_____

How do you feel today?

Date: /   /   Journal Entry

How do you feel today?

Date: /   /   Journal Entry

How do you feel today?

Date: /   /   Journal Entry

Date: / /

Journal Entry

How do you feel today?

Date: / /   Journal Entry

_____
_____
_____
_____
_____
_____
_____
_____
_____
_____
_____
_____
_____
_____
_____
_____
_____
_____
_____
_____

How do you feel today?

Date: /   /   Journal Entry

_____
_____
_____
_____
_____
_____
_____
_____
_____
_____
_____
_____
_____
_____
_____
_____
_____
_____
_____
_____

Date: / /

Journal Entry

How do you feel today?

Date: / /   Journal Entry

How do you feel today?

Date: /   /   Journal Entry

_____
_____
_____
_____
_____
_____
_____
_____
_____
_____
_____
_____
_____
_____
_____
_____
_____
_____
_____
_____

How do you feel today?

Date: / /   Journal Entry

_____
_____
_____
_____
_____
_____
_____
_____
_____
_____
_____
_____
_____
_____
_____
_____
_____
_____
_____
_____

Date: / /

Journal Entry

How do you feel today?

Date: / /   Journal Entry

_____
_____
_____
_____
_____
_____
_____
_____
_____
_____
_____
_____
_____
_____
_____
_____
_____
_____
_____
_____

How do you feel today?

Date: / /   Journal Entry

_____
_____
_____
_____
_____
_____
_____
_____
_____
_____
_____
_____
_____
_____
_____
_____
_____
_____
_____
_____

How do you feel today?

Date: / /   Journal Entry

_____
_____
_____
_____
_____
_____
_____
_____
_____
_____
_____
_____
_____
_____
_____
_____
_____
_____
_____
_____

Date: /   /   Journal Entry

How do you feel today?

Date: / /   Journal Entry

How do you feel today?

Date: /   /   Journal Entry

_____
_____
_____
_____
_____
_____
_____
_____
_____
_____
_____
_____
_____
_____
_____
_____
_____
_____
_____
_____

How do you feel today?

Date: /   /   Journal Entry

___

How do you feel today?

Date: /   /   Journal Entry

_____
_____
_____
_____
_____
_____
_____
_____
_____
_____
_____
_____
_____
_____
_____
_____
_____
_____
_____
_____
_____
_____
_____

How do you feel today?

Date: / /   Journal Entry

Date: /   /   Journal Entry

How do you feel today?

Date: / /   Journal Entry

Date: / /   Journal Entry

Date: /   /
                                                    Journal Entry

How do you feel today?

Date: / /   Journal Entry

_____
_____
_____
_____
_____
_____
_____
_____
_____
_____
_____
_____
_____
_____
_____
_____
_____
_____
_____
_____
_____
_____

Date: /   /   Journal Entry

How do you feel today?

Date: /   /   Journal Entry

_____
_____
_____
_____
_____
_____
_____
_____
_____
_____
_____
_____
_____
_____
_____
_____
_____
_____
_____
_____

How do you feel today?

Date: / /   Journal Entry

___
___
___
___
___
___
___
___
___
___
___
___
___
___
___
___
___
___
___
___
___

How do you feel today?

Date: / /   Journal Entry

How do you feel today?

Date: /   /   Journal Entry

_____
_____
_____
_____
_____
_____
_____
_____
_____
_____
_____
_____
_____
_____
_____
_____
_____
_____
_____
_____

How do you feel today?

Date: / /   Journal Entry

_____
_____
_____
_____
_____
_____
_____
_____
_____
_____
_____
_____
_____
_____
_____
_____
_____
_____
_____

Date: / /   Journal Entry